Contents

moving from employment to employability

In this chapter you will learn about three key ideas: about the changing nature of work, about what we mean by the term 'employability' and why it is important to share your own responses with others you can depend on for advice.

In doing so, you will understand how these changes to employability are affecting you and also understand the future of the concept of work. We will consider the decline and fall of the traditional job and why the relative job security we have become accustomed to in recent history has disappeared. We will examine how the workplace is being restructured in the twenty-first century and, importantly, how you can get ahead in the employment market by understanding these issues and gaining the vital skills, self-knowledge and confidence to move forward.

Understanding the changing nature of work

This book starts with two premises: firstly, that the traditional job pattern has gone and secondly, that the traditional covenant between employer and employee has also gone – both of them for good. The expectations of our parents of lifetime employment (theirs and ours) have disappeared. That does not mean to say that there will be *un*employment, although inevitably there will be some. Rather, it means that while there will be fewer jobs, there will still be work.

For many generations, there has been the passive expectation of becoming an employee – of devoting x hours a week and y years to a particular employer in return for z salary, and a sense of security. Now, there must be much more active selling of the skills, experience and qualities which each individual can offer.

Understanding the future of work

Government figures reveal that the past decade or so has seen fundamental changes in the UK employment scene. There has been an increase in the number of part-time workers (now totalling 28% of all workers), of short-term contracts and of people retiring or being retired early. In some sectors, the percentage of people taking early retirement through ill-health is staggeringly high. In the UK public sector, for example, according to the Pensions Policy Institute (2005) 68% of fire-fighters, 49% of police, 39% of local government staff, 25% of teachers, 23% of NHS staff, 22% of civil servants and 6% of armed service personnel retire before their official retirement age. By contrast, less than 20% of private sector workers retire early through ill-health. At the same time, the proportion of people feeling secure about their job (particularly in the private sector) fell from 96% in 1990 to 43% in 1996.

Overall:

* there has been a reduction in the level of full-time male employment

* there has been an increase in the level of female employment (but not necessarily full-time or permanent)
* there have been fundamental changes in working patterns
* the shift in employment has been away from large employers to small and medium enterprises (SMEs).

What is a job?

The 'job' is a comparatively recent phenomenon. The first Industrial Revolution gave an almost universal understanding of the concept of a job as a social contract into which we enter with an employer to spend an agreed number of hours per week in his/her employment in exchange for a certain sum of money which allows us, within financial constraints, to spend it in the way we wish to pursue a particular lifestyle.

Because we or our parents may always have known a 'job', it is easy to forget that it is not something that has existed from time immemorial and which should always continue to exist as part of our social fabric. In the pre-industrial age, people certainly had work – but they would have looked at you askance if you had suggested that their work would always remain constant throughout their lives and that they would pick up a pension at the end of it. In certain ways these are concepts we are reverting to.

How jobs were invented

It cannot be over-emphasized that the modern concept of the 'job' is something which emerged with the Industrial Revolution. It was something which in a novel way appeared to offer security, compartmentalizing a large part of the day into a known group or sequence of tasks.

Recent experience of the job has been that, for those in a stable employment situation, the employer would ensure employment until retirement age. Yet for many people, there were no programmes of retirement planning. One day they would be in full-time work, the next day without work. Their final day in work would be marked by a party celebrating the loyalty and achievements of the individual, and with the presentation of a gift such as a gold watch to mark the transition from active work to retirement (literally 'withdrawing'). Surely, the symbolism of the gold watch was bizarre — the overtones of value, worth and treasure were also reinforcing the fact that now (perhaps for the first time in the individual's life) time did not matter! Henceforth there would be no fixed schedules or deadlines.

The decline and fall of the job

In the same way that the first Industrial Revolution of the eighteenth and nineteenth centuries had a major impact on people's lives, so too we are undergoing another industrial revolution in the early years of the twenty-first century.

That initial premise of the job was based upon it remaining fixed within a certain and known world. Of course, dependent upon ability, hard work and opportunities, that job might evolve through promotion into a more prestigious and financially rewarding one — but not necessarily a more enjoyable one as we will see in Chapter 4.

What has happened to make job security disappear?

Daily, the numbers of people who realize that there is no such thing as a permanent, secure job swell. While governments may talk of creating more opportunities for employment (and indeed have created some), there is no suggestion nowadays that full-time permanent employment for everyone will return. Indeed, ministers know that to suggest it would be unrealistic, insincere and unworkable given the changes that have and are happening not just nationally but globally.

The reasons for such change are varied and complex and have evolved over different timescales. But, in summary, there are six principal reasons why this has occurred.

1 The development of a global economy

Many of our consumer goods and indeed much of our culture is now global. Wherever you go in the world, you will see young people wearing clothes or footwear with names like Adidas, Levi's or Nike. Whether it is in Europe, the Far East or the Americas, the goods will be the same. Adidas, a German company, produces its branded garments wherever it can obtain the right balance of cost and quality. The country of origin is immaterial. For example, in these post-Rover days, it is difficult to find any British-badged volume car built in Britain with the exception of the Vauxhall Astra (and Vauxhall is part of the US multi-national General Motors). British brand names are built abroad and some Japanese models (e.g. some Hondas, Toyotas and Nissans) are UK-built.

2 Many jobs are at the mercy of changing customer needs

Until the 1970s, in any European port a large number of dock-workers would be required to unload a ship's cargo. Today, most shiploads are containerized, requiring only a small number of highly skilled crane operators to move the container from ship to dockside storage to truck or rail-wagon from the comfort of an insulated cab. It is not that customers are saying 'We don't want to employ dockers' but rather that they want goods transported securely, safely and with the minimum of handling – with consequent savings in time, paperwork and cost.

3 Technology has changed the nature of many businesses and industries

Substantial technological development allows companies to be more productive with fewer staff. Technology can help drive down costs and drive up consistency of quality. For example, motor manufacturers compare their efficiency on a global scale by quoting the number of labour hours it takes to produce a vehicle. The Nissan plant in Sunderland is currently the most productive car plant in Europe.

Take a look in any newspaper, or telephone or online directory for the number of financial services that can be bought 'direct'. From insurance to pensions and investments, many companies have established themselves to capitalize on the public's requirement for simplicity of service, longer opening hours and doing away with the customer's need to complete paperwork. In these 'call centres' employees, wearing a telephone headset and sitting in front of a computer screen, transact customer business. This is predicted to become a major form of employment, with many employees being part-time, working flexible or unsocial hours. In some cases, the growth in business crosses borders – a major US insurer uses a call-centre in the Republic of Ireland staffed by people several thousand miles from both headquarters and customers and a number of UK companies (e.g. National Rail enquiries, some BT customer services and Supanet, the internet provider) use call-centres in India. Likewise, in some cases, the work is not carried out by the company itself but is subcontracted to other companies, which is called ...

4 'Outsourcing' of work

Outsourcing is a rapidly expanding phenomenon whereby many major companies now retain a small core staff for regular operations and buy-in additional expertise and labour on a short-term or consultancy basis as and when it is needed. This way the company can reduce its payroll and on-costs, focusing its efforts on its core purpose. When it needs additional staff, it calls on a pool of people to whom it may pay relatively high consultancy rates to deliver specified services 'just in time'. When the contract finishes and the need no longer exists, the company no longer has to support these people. For example, in the early 1990s, the Ford Motor Company in Britain needed to downsize to retain its competitiveness. This downsizing coincided with Ford's need to invest in new engineering as it had been contracted to build new engines for international use, as well as enhancing its engineering to meet the demands of the recently acquired prestige marques, Jaguar and Aston Martin. Consequently, while the company introduced a programme of redundancy and early retirement for staff over 50, it also created a consultancy base through which it brought back staff on a consultancy basis. They were contracted over a short term for their engineering skills as and when needed but without a long-term commitment.

5 The contingency worker

Work, and hence employment, are dependent upon there being a demand for goods, products or services. If there is a change in consumer needs but no corresponding adaptation or flexibility from the employer, jobs are at risk. Everyone's work depends upon the organization achieving results. Of course, the first staff to go in difficult times will be the temporary, part-time staff but employers the world over might sigh with relief that even well-established, permanent staff can be lost when finances dictate. (Naturally, this can create major problems when economies or companies experience an upturn and don't have the expertise or experience on tap – but that's a separate issue.)

6 A changing mindset

As organizations become aware of their own fluctuating needs and of how their own long-term strategic planning is limited because of external factors, so they have started to buy-in staffing on an 'as and when' basis. These are not unskilled, casual staff brought in by the holiday trade for the peak summer months. The 'new' workforce may:

* be highly intelligent, gifted creative individuals
* be well-qualified and
* have a wide range of experiences and expertise which can be tailored to the specific needs of the organization buying in such consultancy – whether short term or long term.

These are people who know, understand and value their own skills and expertise and can also sell these skills to the appropriate bidder. They put their own personal progression and employability at least on a par with the organization's objectives.

Restructuring the workplace in the twenty-first century

Restructuring organizations was a major activity of the 1990s, although in recent years the focus has changed. Initially, the purpose was to 'downsize' at all costs – to shed excess capacity, labour, plant and sites in order to achieve a 'leaner, fitter structure'. More recently, the focus has been upon business process, performance improvement and to involve and integrate employees in this exercise. In particular, the principal reasons cited for restructuring now tend to be: meeting customer needs, strategic planning and team-working.

Clear lines of accountability are also important and this has been seen in the public sector with changes to pay and conditions such as 'The Agenda for Change' in the National Health Service (NHS) and the restructuring of staff (according to identified teaching and learning responsibilities for teaching staff and the assimilation of grades for non-teaching staff) in state schools across England and Wales. For many staff in both services, this is a new and sometimes alien work ethic.

Flexibility in employment is a key objective – organizations need flexible employees to meet the demands of today's customers for round-the-clock delivery of products and services. This is why some organizations have now introduced **annualized hours** or **job-shares** to give that mutual flexibility. It does not just affect the private sector – many part-time college lecturers will be on annualized hours, with their teaching 'front-loaded' so that they are not needed (or paid) during the summer examination period.

But flexible employees are also needed to be responsive to changing demands, to take on a wider range of roles and tasks, to switch from project to project at short notice and yet be able to hit the ground running. All this requires competence and confidence in skills and qualities which may not have been in demand previously.

Handling the issues – the government response

Such major changes as those outlined mean that governments need to conduct a radical overhaul of the infrastructure of the tax, social security benefits and contributions systems in order to reflect the flexibility and uncertainty in the labour market. For example, in the UK the unfunded liability for public sector pensions is now about £800 billion – which will fall on taxpayers in the decades ahead.

Government figures show that more of us are living longer and that this trend will continue.

Faced with such challenges in strategic, long-term planning for business, health-care, education and other areas of life, governments are asking questions such as:

* How will people's pensions be paid?
* How can there be an equitable pension treatment for those in the private and the public sectors?
* How can the tax system track the variety of activities in which people may be involved?
* How does the school education system shift from preparing pupils with high levels of static academic knowledge to a flexible working and learning environment in which teachers can no longer sincerely say 'Work hard, get your qualifications and you'll get a good job and a secure career'?
* How does the education system respond to individuals' needs for vocational development that doesn't follow the neat pattern of academic years and terms?

Handling the issues – the personal response

For those of us who have been made redundant, 'outplaced', had contracts terminated, reached the end of a fixed-term contract or otherwise been dispensed with, the feelings can initially be complex and difficult. You can feel rejected or marginalized – both personally and professionally; that your professional expertise and experience is not valued and that the organization's values have diverged widely from your own. You can feel that all the hard work over many years, the loyalty, devotion, goodwill, extra hours and effort, the placing of the job or organization above your own personal or family concerns have counted for nought.

You may ask: 'Has the way in which I handled this contract; achieved that target; dealt with that tricky situation; trained those people; implemented this change or become an integral part of the reason that people want to do business with this organization stood for nothing?'

Facing up to the issues

You can sense a range of emotions – not least at the varying degrees of competence with which change management and matters of outplacement have been handled by those who have no conception of the personal feelings of those involved. Indeed, you can question in a professional context the competence of those remaining. 'What valuable skills does X have which I do not possess?' Perhaps X does indeed have specialized skills or a level of competence from which we could all learn. Or perhaps X has been in post so long that it's going to cost too much to make him/her redundant when normal retirement age is just around the corner. Situations like this can be complex and difficult to analyse and cope with on a personal level, particularly when it is unlikely that you will have at your fingertips all the relevant facts upon which corporate decisions have been made.

Increasingly, there is alarm in the UK about the cost of pension provision in the public sector. In an era of people living longer and longer, the number of people active in employment (and who will be called on to pay for the state pension) is diminishing rapidly, putting an estimated additional burden of £30,000 on each household to pay for this provision. In 2010 there were 4.1 British workers per pensioner but there are forecast to be fewer than 3.5 by 2020 and just 2.8 by 2030. (Source: *Daily Telegraph*, 8 May 2010.)

What is clear from the above is that people will have to work longer in order to receive less in pension payments – so we may as well do work we enjoy!

And, of course, we must remember that for some people, the offer of early retirement, voluntary or compulsory redundancy will be eagerly grasped. They have had enough of that organization and are ready for a change, or for a break from or an end to work. They may take away with them a negative attitude to work and are sufficiently comfortably off not to bother with it again. Such people are a dying breed, both in terms of attitude and financial well-being.

But those for whom a new stage in life beckons and who want to approach work in a more pro-active way than previously, this book is going to help build upon those skills and experiences.

Self-check questions

If you have experienced one of the situations described above, it is important to reflect upon and to discuss your personal response. You may already have done so – with former colleagues, in the pub or with friends and family. But many people do not discuss the issues of how they feel. Before we proceed, it is important to get such feelings in the open, otherwise they will be at the back of your mind when we are trying to move forward. You can jot down some points or use the questions as a trigger for a discussion with someone whose opinion and listening skills you value.

If you have been made redundant or outplaced, how do you feel about:

* The way in which it was done?

* How it affects your attitude to work?

* How it affects your attitude to life?

* How it affects your opinion of yourself?

* How you feel about future prospects of work?

2

getting to know yourself — what you are

In this chapter you will consider four key ideas: about what you identify as the key milestones in your own life; about the influences which various people have had on your life and career; about the variety of roles you play across the breadth of your life; and, importantly, how to make a PEST of yourself.

This process will involve getting to know yourself by reflecting upon your life so far; and then identifying those who have influenced you to become the individual you are. We will consider how you can maintain your employability and rate your confidence in your own employability. This is a crucial step if you are going to know what your own relative strengths and weaknesses are and how you can develop those crucial skills for your career.

How did you become what you are today? Whatever stage of life you have currently reached, there have obviously been powerful influences that have brought you to this stage. These might be educational, sociological or anthropological. They might include influences from family, your peer group, previous employers or other sources. It can be enlightening to reflect on these and to consider how they have influenced us to become *what* we have become.

Recalling experiences

For this next activity, picture in your mind two educational experiences you have had – one good and one bad. These experiences can be from any part of formal education at primary, secondary or other education or training. For example, it could be improving your numeracy skills, learning to drive or learning to crochet. It could be a formal learning situation or an informal one. It really doesn't matter as long as you can identify *one* situation in which you feel you learned a lot and *another* in which you feel you learned little.

For instance, taken from school, an example of the first experience might be: 'We had just started algebra and I found the concepts really difficult. The teacher sat down next to me, gave me some individual tuition, patiently explaining it for several minutes. Then everything clicked.'

Or for the second experience, 'One day the teacher left the classroom for a few minutes and, on returning, found that a lot of pupils were playing around. The whole class was put in detention even though I was getting on quietly with the work set.'

Remember that although these experiences are taken from school, your experiences can be from any aspect of your own education or training.

To help you visualize the experience, try to picture the teacher/tutor/trainer in your mind.

Recall experience 1
Recall experience 2

Having recalled both experiences, try now to assess *why* you have recalled them.

* What is it about these two experiences that sticks in your mind?
* What do they tell you about the way you learn or respond to learning?
* What do they tell you about the way you are motivated or demotivated?

Considering your achievements

Frequently, when we think about achievements, we tend to think only in terms of educational achievements (number of exam passes, etc.). Without devaluing the importance of these, they represent only one aspect of our lives. How many other things have we done, perhaps where there has been no formal recognition of our achievements? Examples of achievements outside education might include: learning to swim as an adult, acting as a peacemaker between squabbling family members, redecorating the lounge.

Identifying those who have influenced you

Consider who in *your* life has influenced you, acted as an enabler, opened your eyes or in some way had a lasting impact on the way in which you have evolved. Jot down who these people were and how they may have influenced you in some significant way. If you wish, you can add to the list, but keep it to those who have really had an influence on you.

Those who have influenced you:	How they have influenced you:
....	....
....	....
....	....
....	....
....	....
....	....
....	....
....	....
....	....
....	....
....	....

Self-check questions

* Would those who influenced you understand the situation you are in now?
* What advice would they give you now that you are considering this change in your life?

Identifying what you do

Whatever actions have led us to our current situation, much of our life may now be spent carrying out different tasks in particular roles. We each have different aspects to our total being which cumulatively make us the people we are. What might these different roles be? For example: colleague, line-manager, trade union official, parent, brother/sister, etc. We sometimes use the expression: 'Wearing my ... hat, I think that ...'. Different roles call for different actions and attitudes and these can sometimes cause conflict. For example, we may have to discuss with a colleague his or her work performance and perhaps we have to criticize it – poor punctuality, missing an important meeting, ignoring a deadline, etc. It can be hard to do this, yet it is both expected of us and will certainly cause more trouble if we do not tackle the situation in the early stages before it becomes a real problem.

Yet when that colleague is also a friend, it can be more difficult still. Which hat do we wear – that of friend, colleague or boss? Do we swap hats at stages during the discussion? If, when wearing a manager's hat, we have had to criticize someone, how do we ensure that when we next see him or her at a social gathering that he or she knows we are wearing a different hat? Of course, style of conversation, facial expressions, body language, postural mirroring and context can all give the necessary signals. Even so, making the switch between roles – changing the hats – can cause stress.

Filling in the labels with the roles you hold

Identify your own 'hats' or roles. Here are some examples:

mother	colleague
father	boss
son	manager
daughter	junior
brother	trade union representative
sister	team leader
relative	team member
husband	opposite number
wife	mentor
partner	role model
home maker	coach
cook	paymaster/mistress
taxi driver	appraiser
counsellor	appraisee
mender of broken hearts	student
teacher	contractor
customer/client	

Maintaining your employability

Being a PEST

Predicting the future is an inexact science, to say the least. There can be many factors which bring about or influence changes, as we saw in Chapter 1. A helpful way of trying to assess and understand the likely trends and developments in your own employment sector is to carry out a **PEST analysis**. This may help you get a greater understanding of what is happening and where your organization thinks it is going. Useful sources of information can be company newsletters, news items in the media about your sector, websites and internal memos and notices about changes.

A PEST analysis considers in sequence the various factors that may have an impact upon your sector and your own organization:

* **P**olitical
* **E**conomic
* **S**ocial trends and
* **T**echnological.

Understanding these can give you a clearer sense of that is happening to the organization and, through that, a clearer understanding about your own situation in the workplace.

P
E
S
T

Being a rounded person

People often feel that all that employers are looking for is someone who can carry out a specific role or function within the organization – to wear a particular hat. But, as we have just seen, none of us ever wears just one hat. Some people, particularly the self-employed and those with a portfolio career, are changing hats frequently. Even for those in traditional employment, some jobs require frequent changes. Take a secondary school teacher, for example. Every 35 minutes, he or she will change roles to take a different class, each comprising individual pupils with individual needs; each time the bell sounds the lesson content will be different, needing to be pitched at different levels; every lesson, the group dynamics and class management skills will be varied in order to present an accessible yet challenging learning environment.

Yet, as we can see from the example above, when a school appoints a teacher, it is not merely seeking a teacher of subject X. It is seeking a team member, someone who will volunteer for out of school activities, someone to bring expertise and understanding of children, ideas, equipment, finance or administration as well as subject knowledge. It is all too easy for employees in any field to forget that employers will take the overview of the total contribution to the organization an individual can bring.

Rating your confidence in your employability

How positive or confident do you feel about your employability with your current employer? Read through the table below and score yourself accordingly.

How confident are you about your current employment?

I feel of value and know that my skills and knowledge are in demand. I can see progression opportunities within the organization. Should there be organizational changes I know clearly what I want and am confident of having the right skills to offer. I am confident that I can create and gain fulfilling work within the organization.

Positive

Currently my work and role are valued. I have the necessary skills and aptitudes to perform other organizational roles. My future within this organization is uncertain and I have no clear sense of either who to talk with or what I should do if my post disappears.

Unsure

There is uncertainty about my current post. I worry about the future because I don't think that I have the right contacts, skills or aptitudes to achieve a post I want here. Nevertheless, I recognize that I have plenty to offer and I'm keen to learn.

Anxious

My skills are solely job-specific. If this post goes, I don't know what else I could do. I feel very pessimistic about getting another job with this organization and don't know what they could give me. I have never been encouraged to think about what else I could offer. Is it too late now?

Negative

Now think about how confident you feel about applying for posts with other organizations.

How confident are you about applying for posts with other organizations?

I am alert to the employment market in my sphere. I am confident that I could gain fulfilling work with another organization. I am pro-active and constantly seeking ways to develop my employability and to creating opportunities for myself.

Positive

I have a reasonable understanding of the employment market —
enough to know where my strengths and weaknesses are. I don't
like the idea of change but am sufficiently realistic to grasp the
opportunities offered to me.

Unsure

I have always developed job-specific skills but can see now
that I need to develop a wider range of skills and qualities. I am
concerned that I won't be able to do enough quickly enough to
catch up.

Anxious

When I look around the employment scene I feel that I have little
to offer someone else. My skills and abilities don't seem to be in
demand. I am very worried about not having employability skills.

Negative

Interpreting your response

If your personal confidence rating has been low in either case,
this book will help you enhance your confidence as your skills
develop. If you scored yourself in the top half of the scale, the book
will help you to maintain your employability.

3

getting to know yourself – who you are

In this chapter you will learn: about the significant events which have shaped your life; how to distinguish your real needs from your desires; and how being aware of these factors helps you create the change you are seeking.

So, we'll be looking at *who* you are so that you can start to feel comfortable with being you. In order to do this we'll do some 'life-mapping', which in turn will help you to identify your needs and desires. You'll start to think about what you actually want from life and the steps to take to help this happen. Armed with this knowledge, you can feel more in control of your own situation by being more alert to events around you and spotting opportunities. We'll also ask how you might be remembered as the person you were!

Starting to feel comfortable with being you

So far we have seen some of the major changes affecting the idea of employment and have considered the impact which this has upon people in work. In the last chapter we considered the various factors which have brought you to the position you now occupy as an employee or potential employee (in other words, *what* you are now).

In this chapter we are going to look at some of the factors that have made you the *person* you are today. If we can understand ourselves, we stand a much better chance of finding a working environment that shares those values.

How often when we meet someone do we ask them *what* they do? Even where the discussion is not related to our work or workplace, we often don't converse in general. We gradually move the conversation towards 'jobs', not only to find some common ground but also to see where we may be in the employment 'pecking order'. In Western society we can be obsessed with workplace-based notions of comparative status, and perhaps no country has been as obsessed with this concept as Britain! No wonder other nations have found Britain so class-riddled. As such, our conversations can become stilted by focusing too much on what people are rather than *who* they are as individuals.

In order to consider who you are, you need to reflect on your past life.

Life-mapping

The following activity is a very practical one designed to help you understand how you have reacted to some of the most significant events in your life to date, and how those experiences may affect your response to change now or in the future.

Below is a sample **life-map**, in this case belonging to Ramish, who was asked to identify the most significant events in his life (both positive and negative).

Here is Ramish's list:

1 Enjoyed primary school where I set my sights high.
2 Started secondary school – intimidating atmosphere and made to feel insignificant. Determined to prove teachers wrong.
3 Got good O level results – chose science A levels, intending to read medicine.
4 Grades not good enough to get into medical school. Selected osteopathy at a college.
5 Enjoyed college and socializing.
6 Fell deeply in love with Prakesh, who then rejected me.
7 Got first job and bounced back from disappointment in love by proving competence in work.
8 Death of father. Plunged into grief but eventually emerged with new vigour.
9 Met Mia. Best thing that's ever happened.
10 Promoted into management – frustrated and feeling trapped.

Ramish then plotted these events on a graph, indicating their relative positive or negative rating. His graph is shown in Figure 1.

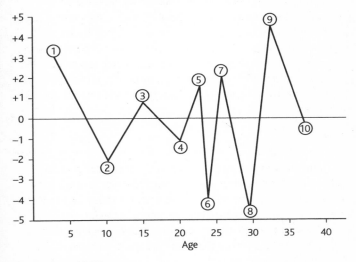

Figure 1 *Ramish's life-map.*

Below is a blank life-map. Complete the table in chronological order with your own significant events – you may need to reflect carefully on some of these as some events will come to mind more readily than others.

Making your own life-map

1
2
3
4
5
6
7
8
9
10

Now complete the numbered events on the grid in Figure 2, adjusting the age scale to your own circumstances.

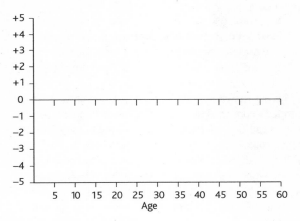

Figure 2 *Life graph for self-completion.*

What does the chart signify?

If we look at Ramish's list of events, we can see a mixture of positive and negative experiences, the degree of positive or negative rating being apparent from its position in the grid. What is noticeable is that, for Ramish, each negative experience is followed by a positive experience. For example, his sense of inferiority at school is accompanied by a determination to do well; his disappointment with his A level results is followed by a successful college course; his rejection in love is countered by the success he found in his work; and the loss of his father enables him to develop new priorities in life. His current situation (frustration in his work and what he gains from it despite his promotion) may be overcome by the closeness of the love and support of Mia who may spur him on to other things.

Your chart may not look like this. Negative experiences may not be mirrored by positive subsequent experiences.

However, look at your negatives where they occur. Ask yourself:

* Did the negative episodes have a learning experience for you?
* If so, what was the positive to emerge from this?
* How did that positive occur – was it just chance or did you make it happen?
* What did the negative experience and your response to it tell you about yourself?

This activity can be helpful in considering how you have responded to previous situations. This is what some football managers call 'bounce-back-ability'). Have you sought shelter from such painful changes by turning your back on everything outside the safe routine you have become accustomed to? Have you embraced the opportunities which change might offer? Have you learnt how you react as an individual in the face of adversity? Do you feel stronger or weaker in the face of such experiences?

Preparing for the future

The next step is to prepare for future situations. The following activity is designed to help you project forwards to enable you to consider how you might want to spend the rest of your life. This is important for assessing your own employability skills because it will help you come to terms with what you want from life, including what you want from work. This activity requires you to think carefully about your dreams, your needs and how you might achieve them. The activity will take you about 20 minutes but you need quiet and to be able to concentrate. You will also need a pen or pencil. (If you are on a train or plane with enough time before your journey finishes, you'll be able to do this.) If you cannot do so at this stage, put the book aside and plan a time when you can complete the task in one go. Don't skip the activity and read ahead – you'll lose out on a crucial step.

Identifying your needs and desires

We often think we know what we really want. Few people would turn down a lottery or pools win. Few of us do not dream of holidaying in some exotic location. But for many people these desires are unachievable. The exotic holiday is part of an imaginary lifestyle. The pools win is a catalyst to a lifestyle rather than a desire in itself. At a more mundane level we might desire a new iPod, the latest wide-screen TV or a ride-on motor lawnmower. All of them are 'merely' materialistic *desires* — we can live without them and most of us do.

What we are considering here is what actually drives our innermost *needs*. For many people, these needs can be independent of financial situation (as long as we are not in poverty). For others, the financial imperative is still there (why do 'fat cats' insist on high bonuses even when they have phenomenally high salaries anyway?). For others, there are more spiritual or literary/artistic drives. Some people need to feel a sense of power or control. Some people are gregarious and always need other humans around them while others prefer a more solitary existence. Some people need precise, ordered systems by which to live their lives, while others prefer an element of disorder. We are all different and no one way is more 'desirable' than another. (We will look at these human needs in more detail again in Chapter 4.)

Listing your needs and desires

To plan the next stages of your life, you need to understand what might be the differences between your desires and your needs.

To help you do this, imagine what you will be doing in the future. Often when we do this, we close our eyes. For obvious reasons you cannot do so now! Nevertheless, try to imagine the next stages of your life and to picture a *typical* day over three timescales.

What will you be doing in 12 months' time?
* What will your life be like?
* What will your work be?
* Who will be the important people in your life?

You may find it useful to jot some points down in the space here.

When you have completed your mental picture, ask yourself: How different is 12 months from today? Is it simply projecting your existing life a year ahead? Maybe you have pictured your children as a year older and at a different phase of their life? Maybe relationships with loved ones have changed. Some of these we might take for granted given the passage of time. But how are *you* different? Have you noted any major or minor shift in you?

What will you be doing in three years' time?
* What will be a good day at work?
* What do you associate with satisfying work?
* What would be a good day outside of work?
* What factors will be absent?

How many of the images you have written down for three years hence are linked with those for 12 months' time? Are there similarities or have you moved on in your thoughts? Perhaps 12 months is too short a timescale to achieve what you really want but there are some glimmers of that achievement over a three-year period. How many of these things have come about by chance and how many because you have been pro-active in making them happen? And if you have been pro-active, when did that process start? What are some of the small, perhaps seemingly insignificant things you have done to cause this to happen? Has it been, for example: planning your activities, prioritizing demands or saying 'no' to people?

What will you be doing in ten years' time?
   * Where will you be living?
   * What might a good day consist of?
   * What experiences would be pleasurable to you?

Has there been any shift in your images over this period of time? It would be extremely unlikely if there had not. Some of these may be dependent upon your age now. How do you get from now to then?

My epitaph

Now, here is your opportunity to confront yourself with how you think people will remember you.

As you consider your own achievements, don't fall into the trap of mere 'conventional' achievements such as just listing your qualifications or projecting your perceived status in terms of job title. They may say *what* you were but not *who* you were. As the old joke goes, very few people die wishing that they had spent more time at the office.

Think also of the things that you had wanted to achieve and believe that you have achieved. Again, this will give you an idea of your values, or what you hold dear in life, of the things which you are prepared to give time and effort to in your life.

You can, if you wish, complete the template below to write about yourself. This is how you see yourself at the moment.

The death of (name) .... (aged) .... has just been announced. S/he is remembered principally for endeavouring to ....
....
....

S/he had always wanted to ....

S/he will be remembered for her/his contributions in the sphere of
....
and will be remembered by .... and ....
.... because of her/his ....
....

If you were to write about yourself in 12 months', three years' and ten years' time, how might the memories of you be different? How much would you have achieved of the, as yet, unfulfilled ambitions and needs?

You can, if you wish, develop this into an open epitaph written on the outline headstone in Figure 3.

IN MEMORY OF

Figure 3 *Analyse your needs and desires by writing your epitaph.*

4

motivation at work

In this chapter you will learn: about some of the main theories of workplace motivation; how to identify what motivates you personally in work and how different employers use a range of strategies to motivate their staff.

In examining motivation at work, we'll ask: what motivates me? We'll check out what some of the key Western experts in workplace and human psychology say in their theories about workplace motivation. You'll be able to match these ideas against what you consider motivates or demotivates you at work. You might be surprised at some of the ideas, or recognize that what you feel is quite widespread. Knowing what makes *you* tick is a vital area of self-awareness. Such knowledge will place you well ahead in the jobs market and will help you target your job search and applications more successfully.

What motivates me?

In the previous chapter you have had an opportunity to consider some of the factors which have made you the person you have become. You have also considered some of the changes which might come about in the future to help you achieve the sort of lifestyle you seek.

Linked with this is an understanding of the sort of things in the workplace that motivate you – in other words, what makes you tick. Different people are motivated by different things, precisely because we are all different. For example, some people thrive on change and constant new challenges. For others, constant change would be very unsettling and, once they have mastered certain tasks performed in a set way, they don't like to see any alteration to this.

Employers can also adopt a variety of approaches to staff motivation, depending on how deeply they understand the needs of the workforce or whether they consider that each employee shares the same motivating forces they do.

In order to understand what motivates people, it can be very illuminating to see what some of the principal organizational psychologists have discovered through their research over the years. We're going to look at some of these findings now.

Elton Mayo – acknowledging the human element

Elton Mayo (1880–1949) and his team of psychologists conducted some famous experiments in the 1920s and 1930s on 20,000 Western Electric employees at their Hawthorne plant in Chicago. These became widely known as the Hawthorne experiments. A series of tests involving changes in working conditions (hours of work, length and frequency of breaks and, ironically, lighting conditions, etc.) were carried out.

The research team noticed that when the adverse changes were explained to staff, and when staff felt involved in the process and felt valued as employees, then any such changes did not reduce production levels. Indeed, production rose to an all-time high and absenteeism reduced by over 80%. Where employees had their conditions changed with no consultation or explanation and where no one attempted to make the employees feel valued, then production and efficiency both dropped. Mayo's team concluded that production levels were influenced by factors other than the physical conditions of work.

What Mayo was *not* saying was that, as long as you are nice to your employees, you can get away with anything. However, he did highlight the importance of the human element – of clarifying with employees the reasons for decisions, of involving them, of taking time to get to know them and explain. In short, by valuing the workforce you are more likely to get more from them – as well as a sense of loyalty, of commitment, of a sense of cohesiveness and self-esteem. Additionally, there will be lower staff turnover and a consequent reduction in staff recruitment and training costs.

Such a 'human relations' approach stressed the importance of work groups, relationships, leadership and personnel management in enhancing motivation and understanding organizational behaviour.

Self-check questions

In your experience of work:
* How often have major changes affecting your work been explained to you?
* How have you felt if such changes have not been explained?
* What strategies do you adopt for informing or explaining changes to your colleagues, suppliers, customers, etc?

Abraham Maslow – satisfying inbuilt needs

Maslow (1908–1970) argued that all people have what he called 'a hierarchy of needs'. In other words, each group of needs is at a different level. He identified these needs as:

* physiological (bodily)
* safety
* social belonging
* esteem
* self-actualization, by which he meant realizing one's own full potential.

These needs can be represented as in the pyramid in Figure 4.

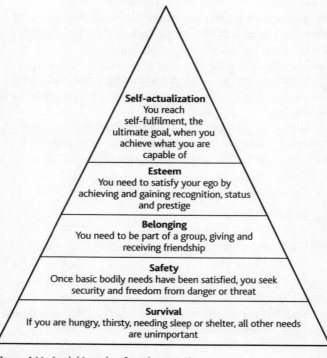

Self-actualization
You reach self-fulfilment, the ultimate goal, when you achieve what you are capable of

Esteem
You need to satisfy your ego by achieving and gaining recognition, status and prestige

Belonging
You need to be part of a group, giving and receiving friendship

Safety
Once basic bodily needs have been satisfied, you seek security and freedom from danger or threat

Survival
If you are hungry, thirsty, needing sleep or shelter, all other needs are unimportant

Figure 4 *Maslow's hierarchy of needs pyramid.*

Maslow's reasoning was that once an individual's physiological needs have been satisfied (warmth, food, etc.), the individual then becomes more concerned with a safe environment. Once this need has been achieved, the individual progresses to concern with a sense of belonging to a community (such as a partner, a family, a social or religious grouping). Beyond this level of need, Maslow argued that individuals need a sense of esteem – of self-worth. They like to feel valued and to have a role or series of roles, whether these are played out in a relationship, in the community or in the workplace. Right at the peak of the pyramid, Maslow contended, was the need for self-actualization – and it is only here that an individual's true potential can be released.

Self-check questions
* When was the last time you were thanked for completing a task well, or on time or under-budget?
* How much scope do you have with your current employer to develop both professionally and personally?
* How far do you agree with Maslow's classification of needs?
* Can you identify any skills or attributes within yourself that you are keen to bring to fruition in the workplace?
* Can you identify any skills or attributes within yourself that you are keen to bring to fruition in your social life?

Douglas McGregor – alternative ways of managing people

Professor McGregor (1906–64), President of Antioch College in Ohio, was influenced by Maslow. He was particularly interested in the way in which managers treated their workforce and how different management approaches determined different responses. He argued that there are essentially two ways of managing and motivating people, and he termed these Theory X and Theory Y.

Theory X is the authoritarian style. This is based on the assumption by managers that people:

* are lazy
* dislike work
* need a mixture of carrot and stick to perform
* are immature
* need direction
* are incapable of taking responsibility for their own actions.

This style of management prevailed, for example, in the British car industry during the 1970s.

Theory Y assumes the opposite. It is based on the assumption by managers that:

* the average human being likes work and gains satisfaction from it
* in the right conditions, people will voluntarily set themselves targets
* encouragement and reward are more effective than threat and punishment
* people learn not only to accept responsibility for their work but will actively seek it.

Japanese-owned or -influenced car industries reflect this approach with employee involvement through 'quality circles'.

Of course, we must recognize that effective management involves sophisticated and complex tasks requiring a range of approaches and styles to be deployed. Even the most enlightened and ardent advocate of Theory Y recognizes that, in order to ensure quality and consistency, you have to be firm and demanding on occasions.

Self-check questions

* Considering your current (or past) employment, in what ways have you experienced a Theory X manager?
* Considering your current (or past) employment, in what ways have you experienced a Theory Y manager?
* In which employment culture do you work better, X or Y?

Frederick Herzberg – identifying the sources of motivation and demotivation

Working with his research colleagues, Herzberg (1923–2000) interviewed more than 200 engineers and accountants in the United States in the late 1950s. They discovered that there was a great similarity in the aspects of their work that these employees found motivating or demotivating. These are shown in the 'content theory' of motivation chart.

Sources of job satisfaction (Motivation factors)	Sources of job dissatisfaction (Demotivation factors)
1 Achievement	1 Company policy/administration
2 Recognition	2 Supervision
3 Work itself	3 Salary
4 Responsibility	4 Interpersonal relations
5 Advancement	5 Working conditions

For many people, the sources of job satisfaction (**motivation factors**) are powerful. Even small elements of these factors can make a significant difference to the way they feel about and respond to work. The sources of job dissatisfaction (**demotivation factors**) are often areas over which the individual has traditionally had little control, the climate and culture of the organization dictating the working practices.

Herzberg argued that simply giving a pay rise would not solve the underlying problems. The pay rise would rapidly become the norm and the real problems would remain.

Self-check questions
* How does your personal list of motivation factors compare with those identified by Herzberg?
* How does your personal list of demotivation factors compare with those identified by Herzberg?

5

understanding what you have to offer

In this chapter you will learn: what the phrase 'transferable skills' means and why these are important; how you can identify and develop your own transferable skills; how it can be really helpful to become a SWOT for the jobs market; and how to describe your own personality.

You will gain a clear understanding of what you have to offer to employers and will also understand what employers themselves seek. This will help you to identify and develop your own transferable skills. In doing so, you will become a SWOT by using a special tool for analysis. You'll then be able to compare your own results with what others think and say about you. You are then set for being in a much stronger position for making job applications and handling job interviews.

Understanding what employers seek

The early chapters of this book have reinforced the idea that the old covenant between employer and employee has been broken for good and that *your future lies in your employability*. It is not up to employers to provide that which they can no longer do – the onus is very clearly on the employee, on you, to make yourself employable in this fast-changing and increasingly complex world.

By this stage, you should also have a clearer understanding of:
* what makes you what you are (Chapter 2)
* what makes you who you are (Chapter 3)
* what motivates or de-motivates you (Chapter 4).

We are now going to consider, firstly, the *skills* and, secondly, the *qualities* you have to offer.

Developing your transferable skills

Transferable skills are those skills which we can take with us from job to job, from task to task or from context to context. They can serve us well in life and are skills which we develop throughout our lives – there is never a stage when we become absolutely perfect communicators, for example. We refine and enhance those skills constantly through practice and by facing new situations and challenges.

In today's working environment, it is essential to be able to use a wide variety of skills and to have the confidence to do so. We need to be able to offer such a range of skills to potential employers or clients, as well as to our existing ones in order to ensure that we are able to undertake work of the highest quality, which is both challenging and fulfilling to us personally.

Employers are becoming much more specific and demanding in terms of the skills they seek. It is no longer enough to approach an employer saying 'I've got three A levels' or 'Here's my degree certificate in Biochemistry'. Whatever the level of employment and the nature of the work, employers need people who can:
* work as part of a team
* communicate effectively in a variety of ways

* be confident problem-solvers
* take on a variety of complex tasks.

Employers are very positive about these skills, as they provide the sort of skill-set and mindset for a flexible and adaptable workforce. Many learners also have responded well to the challenges, particularly where they have developed them through project work. Universities, too, value the skills, given that students these days have to work far more independently than previously, need to access a variety of information in traditional and electronic format with confidence and are often required to make presentations. In some disciplines (e.g. medicine), students' ability to communicate effectively, to work as part of a team and to have skills in problem-solving form an important part of the skill-set needed to actually gain a place at university.

But not everyone has had the opportunity to gain such skills formally and some, particularly those who have been in the workplace longer, may see new recruits with these skills as a threat. So what can you do to recognize and develop your own transferable skills?

Identifying your transferable skills

We do not always know what we are good at. Our families, teachers or employers have not always given us feedback on our strengths, perhaps assuming that we already recognize them. Likewise, unless someone actually identifies and names a skill, we don't necessarily realize that's what it is, what it's called or what we can do!

A comprehensive checklist of transferable skills follows. Don't be horrified by the extent of them – anyone who can claim to have all of these skills developed to a high standard deserves a halo. Nevertheless, it can be extremely useful to understand what these highly sought skills might be, and also to consider how many of these we have and how we have developed them. Increasingly, employers may seek in written applications and at interview a self-awareness of such skills and qualities. Likewise, if you are thinking of going into self-employment, it is essential to have a clear sense of your skills and limitations. You will need an acute awareness of this in order to market your services or products, as well as marketing yourself. We'll look at this aspect in more detail in Chapter 7.

Comprehensive checklist of transferable skills

	Basic level (✔)	High level (✔)	Experiences which have developed these skills (✔)
Problem-solving			
* define and identify the core of a problem			
* investigate what resources are available			
* enquire and research into the available resources			
* analyse data/information			
* show independent judgement of data/information			
* relate data/information to its wider context			
* data appreciation: draw conclusions from complex arrays of data			
* organize and synthesize complex and disparate data			
* apply knowledge and theories			
* show flexibility and versatility in approach			
* use observation/perception skills			
* develop imaginative/creative solutions			
* use an approach sensitive to needs and consequences			
* show resourcefulness			
* use deductive reasoning			
* use inductive reasoning.			

	Basic level (✓)	High level (✓)	Experiences which have developed these skills (✓)
Team-work			
* listen to others			
* be aware of own performance			
* observe others' performance and use perceptions			
* lead and motivate others			
* show assertiveness (set own agenda)			
* co-operate with others			
* negotiate and persuade			
* constructively criticize			
* produce new ideas or proposals			
* clarify, test or probe others' ideas or proposals			
* elaborate on own/others' ideas or proposals			
* summarize – bring ideas together			
* give encouragement to others			
* compromise, mediate, reconcile individuals and/or ideas.			
Managing/organizing			
* identify what tasks need to be done and the timescales involved			
* evaluate each task			
* formulate objectives, bearing in mind those evaluations			
* plan work to achieve objectives/targets			
* carry out work required			
* evaluate and review progress and reformulate objectives			
* cope and deal with change			
* withstand and deal with pressures			

(Contd)

	Basic level (✓)	High level (✓)	Experiences which have developed these skills (✓)
* ensure appropriate resources are available			
* organize resources available			
* show initiative			
* manage time effectively			
* demonstrate sustained effort			
* make quick, appropriate decisions			
* show personal motivation			
* execute agreed plans.			
Communication (oral and written)			
* explain clearly			
* deal effectively with conflicting points of view			
* develop a logical argument			
* present data clearly and effectively			
* take account of audience/reader in oral presentation/writing			
* show evidence of having assimilated facts			
* give appropriate examples			
* show enthusiasm and interest			
* show critical reasoning			
* use appropriate presentation techniques			
* compare and contrast effectively			
* listen and query where necessary			
* discuss ideas, taking alternatives into account			
* defend a point of view			
* assess own performance.			

As you read through the list, score yourself on how well-developed these skills are. Note down also the tasks or experiences which have given you these skills. These may be from your working life or from other activities. For example, being secretary of a local charity may have made you good at 'investigating what resources are available'; being a mother may mean you show 'flexibility and versatility in approach'; or being a trade union representative may have made you able to 'listen to others'. We will return to your responses to this activity in the next chapter. But for now, let's move from thinking about skills to the personal qualities you have as an individual.

Becoming a SWOT

To consider the qualities you have to offer, you are going to have to become a SWOT – but not in the old, school sense. You are going to carry out an activity which every business does in order to identify where it is now and where it is going. By now you should have realized that you are a business – what is sometimes called 'me plc' – the most precious and valuable business you will ever be involved in.

However, your **SWOT analysis** is a breakdown of the **s**trengths, **w**eaknesses, **o**pportunities and **t**hreats of your particular situation as a worker. It is what *you* have to offer. It is about you personally, whereas the PEST analysis you did in Chapter 2 was about your employment sector.

The strengths and weaknesses are *internal* – your inner qualities; while the opportunities and threats are the *external* factors in which you operate – your working environment.

The idea is to honestly and openly appraise your own strengths and weaknesses (SW) and to consider the situation you find yourself in (OT). Positive aspects are on the left-hand side of the SWOT chart (Figure 5), negative aspects are on the right.

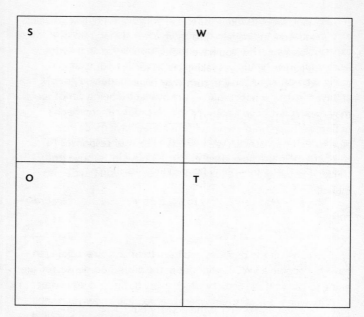

S	W
O	T

Figure 5 *Blank SWOT chart.*

Devising your own SWOT

Having seen how the process of devising a SWOT analysis works, now is the opportunity for you to devise your own. Think about the issues we have discussed in the previous chapters and your own response to these. To help you:

* Be prepared to take some time to devise your SWOT and to revise it in the light of reflection and discussion. The whole process might take you some days – even weeks.
* Identify someone/several people with whom you can discuss your SWOT. Choose people close to you whose opinion you value and who will give you an honest appraisal. This is not the time for false praise.
* Don't underestimate the power and value of this critical support.

* Think about as many aspects of your life as possible (the hats you wore in Chapter 2) to arrive at a rounded view of yourself.
* Assess whether you have the will-power to deal with the negatives as well as taking credit for the positives.
* Identify how you can turn your negatives into positives.

Describing yourself

In carrying out the SWOT analysis you have had to think about the sort of person you are. You have had to describe yourself. That is something that many people find difficult to do because they are not used to being self-critical.

Take the opportunity now to describe yourself *in three words only*, as:
* an employee
* a colleague
* a partner
* a family member
* a human being.

Take as long as you need for the activity but don't agonize over choices – a gut reaction may be more accurate. Fill in your responses next to each category.

My self-description (three words only per category)

* an employee

* a colleague

* a partner

```
    *  a family member



    *  a human being
```

When you are ready to move on, compare the list of words in
Figure 6 with what you have written about yourself.
   * Is there anything that you would add to your lists?
   * Is there anything you would amend?
   * Where there are 'different sides of the same coin'
     (e.g. 'perfectionist' and 'pedantic'), which is the more
     accurate for you?

creative	adventurous	numerate
sensitive	thorough	cautious
organized	eccentric	able to plan long-term
prudent	aggressive	a bully
dynamic	extrovert	can see potential in people
assertive	gregarious	fair
patient	methodical	a good negotiator
flighty	compassionate	able to take an overview
persuasive	unpredictable	good interpersonal skills
generous	polite	self-aware
punctual	profligate	persistent
competitive	nit-picking	pedantic
quick-thinking	charismatic	financially astute
ambitious	loyal	prepared to take a gamble
timid	ruthless	unbiased
inconsistent	leader	sexist
single-minded	enthusiastic	able to plan short-term
cynical	reliable	egotistical

determined	flexible	authoritative
perfectionist	trustworthy	good time-manager
dependable	overbearing	able to delegate

Figure 6 *Words for self-description exercise.*

Reduce this list to three words which, in any situation, you feel summarize your character most accurately. These are the words you can live with if they were to appear on a badge you wore. Transcribe these words on to your 'badge' (Figure 7) and keep them in mind as we go through the rest of the activities.

Figure 7 *Your self-description badge.*

6

developing your skills

In this chapter you will learn: about the crucial importance of a range of skills: communication skills, team-work and other skills. You will also learn how you can enhance your own skills-set.

In doing this, you'll be able to develop your skill-set so that you have a wide range of desirable skills and qualities to offer employers – or to start your own business. We'll explore how you will be able to offer more than qualifications and experience; how communicating effectively is a crucial skill. Finding people in your chosen employment sector to network with is an important skill.

We'll reflect on how good you are at team-working and how you can identify and seize opportunities to enhance your skills.

Communicating effectively

We communicate principally through the four means listed in the following table:

	Learned	Used	Taught
Listening	First	45%	Least
Speaking	Second	30%	Next least
Reading	Third	16%	Next most
Writing	Fourth	9%	Most

What strikes you as odd about this chart? The skill areas we teach are those forms of communication we use least (on average in Western society)! Of course, there will be exceptions – for example, people whose work depends upon frequent and sustained written communication. It is also true to say that the written communication of, say, a job application form or letter of application are perhaps some of the most important communications we make. But in ordinary social interactions, the degree to which we use a particular means of communication is in inverse proportion to its apparent importance of being taught.

As you can see, we are very rarely *taught* to listen yet we spend more of our time listening to other people than we do in any other form of communication. Perhaps because we can *hear* in the womb it is assumed that we know how to *listen*. Is it any surprise that we can often get things wrong? How often have you heard people say of others, 'He's a poor listener' or 'She never hears what I say'? Of course, we never say it about ourselves! In general, perhaps we do not listen as well as we could. List all the people you know who have been fired for listening too well!

Networking

What does networking mean? It means establishing who the likely opinion-formers and influential people in your preferred work sector are; it means getting to know individuals and starting to form relationships with them. Of course, no one likes individuals who force their way into a conversation, full of their own importance and of what they have to offer the world. Such an approach is likely to be counter-productive. But you have to be confident and assertive. If you are not confident of what you have to offer, why should anyone else have faith in you, your specialist skills or knowledge, your product or your service?

Here are some suggestions for ways to network:

* Identify the professional or trade groupings you need to work with and how they operate (conferences, trade fairs, etc.)
* Pick up the phone to likely contacts and make your name known.
* Be persistent but not aggressive.
* Generate interest – once you have one contact, word of mouth can make the effect snowball.
* Start small and work up – if you have a product to sell at, say, a local farmers' market, the big supermarkets are likely to be more interested than if you have no customer base.
* Take calculated risks – if you attend just one convention, you will find out who the movers and shakers are, whether you have a niche expertise, product or service and whether you are cut out for such an endeavour, be a business or a promoted post.
* Develop your emotional intelligence.

Many of the above suggestions will apply to making contacts in your preferred employment sector also.

How good are you at team-working?

At work you will often work with groups of others. Sometimes you might work with a team. What is the difference between a group and a team? Try to write a definition of a team in the following box.

```
A team is ...



```

We all know what a team is in a sporting sense – a band of people with the same aims and goals, with complementary strengths and skills. The same is true of the workplace. Just as you don't expect in a sports team that all team members can excel in one particular aspect (e.g. all rugby players to be fast, light players on the wing, able to outrun their opponents rather than having a more supporting role, literally adding weight to the team), so different skills are necessary in the workplace.

Indeed, it is now accepted that in virtually all jobs, being an effective team-player is essential. Today's working world is too complex for the traditional workplace divisions and demarcations to operate. Many agencies operate multidisciplinary teams (e.g. in social work or health-care) so that holistic care and support is offered to a client/patient. Team-working skills are particularly important in small- and medium-size enterprises (SMEs) where employees can wear many different hats during the working day. Even freelancers have to have effective team skills because, at times, they may be working collaboratively with other freelancers. Many broadcasters are freelance and, if you have ever been in a television or radio studio, you will know that a broadcast depends upon high levels of team-work to ensure smooth transmission – the director, producer, floor-manager, sound and lighting engineers all have to know exactly what others are doing so that they can work effectively.

Defining a team

A team has:
* a clear purpose
* clear, shared aims
* clear sense of individual roles
* strong leadership.

Team-working with colleagues

Take a moment now to reflect on your work over the past week.
* Think of the people you have worked with
* Think of your role/s and of their roles

Now consider: 'In my dealings with all these people over the past week, to what extent have I been working as part of a group and to what extent have I been working in a team?'.

List the group events:
*
*
*

List the team events:
*
*
*

How good do you think you are at being a team player?

Below are some of the key characteristics of team-working:
* able to take instructions
* aware of own role
* aware of team's aims
* aware of team's purpose
* able to support team members
* able to contribute fully to the work of the team;

and of the leader:
* able to lead a team
* able to gain the trust, support and respect of team members
* able to make decisions
* able to delegate authority.

The management writer R. Meredith Belbin, in his famous book *Management Teams: Why They Succeed or Fail*, determined from his research that there were certain key qualities in effective teams. It makes fascinating reading, but essentially he noted that successful teams contain:

* a **co-ordinator**: chairs effectively, is able to get the most from team members, orchestrates the actions of others
* a **doer**: a reliable person who sees actions through, can be prone to perfectionism
* a **thinker**: a strategist – perhaps better at thinking of applications and implications than actually doing
* a **supporter**: reliable, can always be counted on to be there and do things, likes to create a co-operative atmosphere
* a **challenger**: gets the team thinking about what it's doing, perhaps rather prickly and not easily satisfied.

Belbin uses different terminology from the above simplification. He stresses that a team should comprise a number of different personality traits, as above. If all the team members have the same traits, or if these different roles are not included in the team, the team will fail to meet its objectives. Too many people are trying to do the same thing in the same way, or there are gaps in roles or insufficient challenge to perform effectively.

Seizing opportunities to enhance your skills

Whatever your line of work, there will be opportunities to enhance your employability skills. Remember that these are skills which have a value to your current employment as well as to yourself, so seeking to enhance them will also benefit your current employer. You don't necessarily have to look too far – remember that in many aspects of our working life there are positive opportunities and challenges masquerading as insurmountable problems.

Opportunity	Gain
Attending meetings	Discussion/debating/chairing skills
Making a presentation (e.g. to colleagues)	Verbal skills
Taking minutes of meetings	Writing skills
Writing reports	Writing skills
IT skills	Computer literacy/expertise
Organizing an event	Organizational/budgeting skills
Team membership	Team-work skills
Team management	Management/leadership skills
Training a colleague	Training/mentoring skills

The table above is only a short list of possibilities. There will certainly be others which you can identify.

7

assessing your attitude to life

In this chapter you will learn: how to gauge your own attitude to life; about the aspects of working life which you value and about the key decisions you can take for your own future.

In assessing your attitude to life you will start to recognize yourself and to identify your personal values. Determining whether you are an optimist or a pessimist is a good starting point because that affects your own outlook and also the way in which you interact with others. We will also be exploring two increasingly important concepts: the ideas of multiple intelligences and of emotional intelligence. You might be surprised how these can be helpful in work.

This level of self-awareness will focus and enhance your job search.

What is your attitude to life?

How do your friends describe you? As a realist, an optimist, a pessimist or a cynic? They may not necessarily know the 'real' you but others' views can be accurate. More importantly, if your proposed future life involves an element of risk, you need to be of a particular disposition. If your anticipated future career is as a self-employed underwater tap-dancer, you would need certain qualities and attributes: the ability to swim and dive, the ability to look aesthetically pleasing in your actions, to have powerful lungs and all-round fitness. But on top of this you would need optimism that your endeavours would succeed in attracting a sufficiently large audience and to be a risk-taker, not only physically but also financially. If you are temperamentally ultra-cautious, then no matter what your ambition is, you should forget the project. It just wouldn't work for you.

Establishing your own outlook on life is vital in thinking about which direction to take for the future. Let's carry out a few activities to demonstrate this.

Activity 1

Look at the following well-known proverbs. Indicate whether you agree or disagree with these:

		Yes	No
1	You can't have the penny and the bun.	☐	☐
2	What you gain on the swings, you lose on the roundabouts.	☐	☐
3	God helps those who help themselves.	☐	☐
4	All's well that ends well.	☐	☐
5	Don't count your chickens before they're hatched.	☐	☐
6	You learn something new every day.	☐	☐

Activity 2

Look at the pairs of well-known proverbs and phrases below. Tick the one that is most in tune with your philosophy or outlook on life.

1	You're never too old to learn.	☐
2	You can't teach an old dog new tricks.	☐
3	No smoke without fire.	☐
4	Every cloud has a silver lining.	☐
5	If something can go wrong, it will.	☐
6	It'll be alright on the night.	☐
7	Many hands make light work.	☐
8	Too many cooks spoil the broth.	☐
9	Look before you leap.	☐
10	Nothing ventured, nothing gained.	☐

Activity 3

Look at the illustration below. What do you see?

Assessing your answers

What were your responses to these activities?

* *Activity 1*: Proverbs 3, 4 and 6 are optimistic, while 1, 2 and 5 are pessimistic.
* *Activity 2*: Proverbs 1, 4, 6, 7 and 10 are optimistic, while 2, 3, 5, 8 and 9 are pessimistic.
* *Activity 3*: To you, was the bottle half-full or half-empty?

If you erred towards the more pessimistic interpretations of the above, then maybe you are by nature a pessimist or cynic. If you erred towards the optimistic, then that is likely to be your disposition.

Personality

Is it possible to 'measure' an individual's personality? Certainly, we can identify specific personality traits, but ultimately each individual's personality is unique. One of the best-known personality tests is the Myers-Briggs Type Indicator®. This is a self-report questionnaire based on the theory of psychological type developed by Carl Jung. The questionnaire was developed by Katherine Cook Briggs and Isabel Briggs Myers and, worldwide, over 3.5 million such indicators are undertaken annually. In essence, it identifies individuals' preferred responses in a range of situations, dividing people into extroverts and introverts. It's important to recognize what these terms mean — it is more sophisticated than the commonly held belief that introverts are shy and extroverts are outgoing.

What is crucially important also is that the test does not suggest that particular personality types are 'better' than others. To do so would simply suggest that there is a desired template we should all strive for and that is nonsense. But it is helpful to know the general way in which we are likely to respond to certain situations — the areas in which we feel comfortable (our 'comfort zone') and those we may prefer to avoid or in which we lack confidence. People who have undertaken such questionnaires generally comment on the extraordinary level of accuracy of the results and how they have helped them to understand their workplace behaviour.

Knowing what suits you

Assessing what suits you

* If a set routine, a known and regular income and being able to take for granted all the infrastructure of a large organization is important to you, would you be able to

work for a small organization where a variety of roles are expected, or work for yourself?

* If your list comprises mostly negative factors, where will a more positive working environment be found?

* If your current work offers a mixture of positive and negative factors, can you identify which ones you could take with you and which ones you would be happy to leave behind?

Multiple intelligences

Do you remember the activity you undertook at the beginning of Chapter 2, about positive and negative learning experiences? That illustrated some of the aspects and approaches to learning you valued or which you found difficult. Your response had nothing to do with your 'intelligence'. Indeed, these days, it is recognized that the traditional view of intelligence and measuring it by IQ is very limited and inaccurate. People learn in a wide variety of ways from a multitude of experiences and through a variety of their senses.

The psychologist Howard Gardner recognized this and devised the term 'multiple intelligences'. Gardner identified different intelligences, as illustrated in Figure 8.

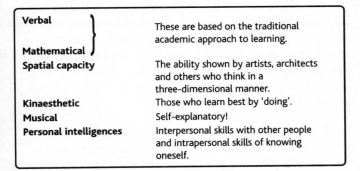

Verbal ⎫	These are based on the traditional academic approach to learning.
Mathematical ⎭	
Spatial capacity	The ability shown by artists, architects and others who think in a three-dimensional manner.
Kinaesthetic	Those who learn best by 'doing'.
Musical	Self-explanatory!
Personal intelligences	Interpersonal skills with other people and intrapersonal skills of knowing oneself.

Figure 8 *Howard Gardner's 'multiple intelligences'.*

Having a sense of how you learn best is clearly helpful. As we are seeing, it has a strong influence on the type of work in which you feel most fulfilled.

Emotional intelligence

Emotional intelligence is a relatively new term, based on the work of the American author Daniel Goleman, and is an extension of the multiple intelligences work of Gardner. There are five components of Emotional Intelligence (sometimes called EI):

* **Self-awareness:** This is exhibited by self-confidence, realistic self-assessment and a self-deprecating sense of humour.
* **Self-management:** This is exhibited by trustworthiness and integrity, comfort with ambiguity and openness to change.
* **Self-motivation:** This is exhibited by a strong desire to achieve, optimism and high organizational commitment.
* **Empathy:** This is exhibited by expertise in building and retaining talent, cross-cultural sensitivity, and service to client and customers.
* **Social skills:** This is exhibited by the ability to lead change efforts, persuasiveness, and expertise in building and leading teams.

Goleman argues that emotional intelligence is particularly relevant in jobs requiring a high degree of social interaction.

In essence, many of the activities you have undertaken while reading this book have been covered by the above aspects. Certainly, you will have a higher degree of self-awareness; and in making your choices you are displaying self-management, based upon a greater understanding of what motivates you. The activities in developing your transferable skills have focused on social, team and influencing skills and towards sensitivity to others as well as yourself.

Checking the lifeboat

By now you are beginning to get a feel for what best suits you. You need to take into account a number of factors:

* your temperament
* your aspirations
* your skills
* your experience
* your qualities
* your individual situation.

There are times when we have to make uncomfortable decisions about our working life and employment, yet at the same time be comfortable with living with the consequences of those same decisions.

If you stay where you are
* There may still be uncomfortable times ahead.
* Things may not get better.
* At least it is a known environment and situation.
* 'Better the devil you know than the one you don't'.

If you 'jump'
* Do you know where you are heading?
* Is it 'out of the frying pan into the fire'?
* Is it 'a leap in the dark'?
* Or is it a question of 'jumping ship before it goes down'?
* Or of jumping before you are pushed?
* Can you accept an element of risk?
* What element of risk can you accept?
* Can you live with the consequences of the decision – good and bad?

We have seen that life, by its very nature, involves change. Both our attitude to change and our attitude to others are based on our perception of them. In order to genuinely move forward, we have to understand ourselves, our attitude to risk and how far we wish to take control of situations rather than allowing situations or long-standing custom and practice to control us.

And if by the time you reach the end of this book, you are genuinely happy with 'what you've always got', that is fine.

8

where are you going next?

In this chapter you will learn: which planning techniques can help you to plan your own future; how to develop some generic employability skills; and about the core elements of creating satisfying work for yourself.

Many people can have time management concerns – which in turn cause work-related stress. To help address the issue of managing time, we will identify whether you have a time management problem, and consider issues like avoiding procrastination, prioritizing activities and reducing them to manageable chunks.

We'll identify what makes you stressed and reveal some tips on how to manage stress. We'll consider how to market yourself whether for employment or self-employment and thus maintain your employability.

Managing time

Managing time is a constant source of pressure for many people who feel that they have too many responsibilities for the time available. Some people are better time managers than others – they like to be organized, can prioritize, can project ahead and work backwards by allocating tasks to meet specific deadlines. But, whether you are looking to change employment sector, gain promotion or work for yourself, everyone can gain from better time-management skills. So how do yours rate?

Start at the beginning

A good starting place for developing your own time management skills is to consider the main tasks in your job/role. This will vary according to whether you are in full- or part-time work, your domestic situation, etc. In other words, you need to identify what tasks your work involves. What tasks do you have to get done in order to meet your employment/study/family commitments?

In the box below, list the main tasks of your work. Group them together so that there are a maximum of ten.

1

2

3

4

5

6

7

8

9

10

Matching size of task to importance

The circle below represents the entirety of your work. Using the list of tasks you identified above, allocate each task a segment of the circle according to its importance in your mind for carrying out your work. For example, if you consider that writing up the sales figures of your department is the single most important aspect of your work, you will allocate it the largest segment. (All segments should be as accurate as possible but don't worry about geometrical precision!)

Points to consider:

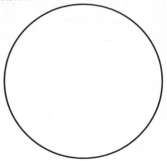

* Are there any discrepancies between what you consider to be the most important tasks and the amount of time you spend on them?
* Are there any tasks about which you feel rushed or pressurized for time?
* Are there any tasks or responsibilities on which you spend too much time for their overall importance?

Do I have a time management problem?

How do you fare in this questionnaire? Read the numbered statements and then rate according to the column headings.

		Very often	Quite often	Sometimes	Rarely or never
1	I can't get on with my work because of interruptions outside my control.				
2	The meetings I attend could be better organized.				
3	Problems I have not foreseen interfere with my work.				
4	Colleagues take my time without making an adequate contribution to my effectiveness.				
5	I waste the time of others with whom I work.				
6	I find tasks to keep busy, avoiding things I should be doing.				
7	Poorly designed systems in the organization waste my time.				
8	I keep my work in piles on the desk, on shelves, by the phone etc.				
9	I put off big or difficult jobs.				
10	I waste time looking for files, papers, etc.				
11	Meetings take up too much of my time.				
12	I have my diary/organizer with me.				

	Very often	Quite often	Sometimes	Rarely or never
13 Most of my time is under my control.				
14 I set a priority for each piece of work I do.				
15 I organize my workspace/office in a systematic manner.				
16 I list tasks on a 'to do' list to keep my priorities before me.				
17 Decisions and actions are followed up promptly.				
18 I ask myself: 'Am I working on the right thing in the right way at the right time?'				

Procrastination

Procrastination – or putting things off – is the most commonly indulged-in time-waster. We all do it to a lesser or greater degree. The key point is to be able to identify when and why we are doing it.

Do you recognize any of these factors in yourself? This is well worth asking and being *totally honest* with yourself. If you intend becoming self-employed you really do need to recognize this quality and what you can do about it – otherwise, it will cost you time and, literally, money.

Reasons for procrastination
* You think the task is unpleasant, overwhelming, not fun, outside your 'comfort zone', or a risk.
* You don't know where or how to start.
* 'There isn't time.'
* You won't be able to do the job perfectly.
* You think the job's too big – you can do lots of little jobs in the same time.

Some suggestions to help with procrastination

Completing the table below will help you to identify ways of dealing with time wasting and procrastination.

Time-waster	Possible causes	Ways to overcome	My improvement plan
Taking phone call after phone call	'Politeness'	Use voicemail/ answering machine to screen calls	Switch on voicemail when I have important tasks to do
Email	Feel I have to reply as soon as mail comes in	Prioritize responses	Reply in batches

Prioritizing

At the start of any given day, make a written list of the tasks facing you – this is always good practice anyway. Think of all those tasks as an archer's target, as shown in Figure 9.

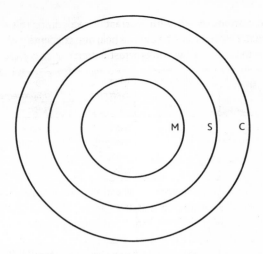

Figure 9 *The must, should and could do target.*

Divide your tasks into three categories:

* Tasks which you **must** do **(M)**. These are important, urgent and non-negotiable tasks. Failing to complete them will cause major inconvenience for yourself, colleagues, customers or suppliers. There is no way you can avoid these tasks.
* Tasks which you **should** do **(S)**. These are less important and less urgent than those at the centre of the target. You can delay these until you have the M tasks completed. However, if you delay them too long, they will simply become 'must do' tasks. Plan ahead and aim to complete (or at least make a start) on these before they become urgent.
* Tasks which you **could** do **(C)**. These are currently unimportant and time devoted to them will only detract from completing other more important tasks. Indeed, you might ask yourself 'What would be the consequence of not doing this task?' If there is no significant problem, why do it anyway?

Don't fool yourself that there is nothing that you can omit or that is less important than others. If some tasks are more important, it follows that others are less important. In recognizing this, you are prioritizing and are on your way to managing your time.

The ability to separate urgency and importance is vital to effective time management. The following matrix is useful to distinguish between tasks:

Urgent and important	**Urgent** but not important
Important but not urgent	Neither important nor urgent

* Tasks which are '**urgent and important**' need your immediate and full attention.
* Those which are '**urgent** but not important' need immediate attention but could be dispatched quickly.
* Those which are '**important** but not urgent' need addressing fully in time.
* Those which are 'neither important nor urgent'– why are you even considering doing them?

The 4Ds alternative approach

An alternative to the above approach is the 4Ds. Make a list of all the things you have to do. Then put them into the appropriate boxes in Figure 10.

Do	Delegate
Delay	Dump

Figure 10 *4Ds matrix template for self-completion.*

* The list in the **do** box should get smaller as you get better at time management.
* **Delegate** where you can (or dump and see how important it was).
* Use the **delay** box to park things briefly while you deal with the do box — but don't let it get urgent!
* **Dump** trivial things even if you want to do them.

Reducing tasks to a manageable size

Strategies for enhancing your time management should include focusing on breaking down a large task into its smaller component chunks. Such 'chunking' allows the task to be more manageable. There are two ways of doing this: (1) pizza slicing and (2) nibbling.

Pizza slicing

As shown in Figure 11, this approach goes right to the heart of the problem, undertaking a manageable chunk at a time. You might liken this approach to some aspects of gardening. You identify a part of the garden that needs attention and then do everything in that area: cutting back undergrowth, weeding, digging the soil over, replanting, etc. The rest of the garden needs doing but you've made a substantial impact in that one area.

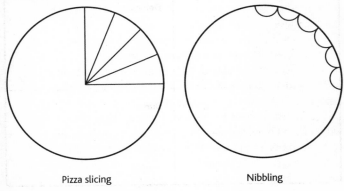

Pizza slicing   Nibbling

Figure 11 *Pizza slicing and nibbling, to reduce tasks to a manageable size.*

Nibbling

As the name suggests, this involves taking small, bite-sized chunks at a time, gradually reducing the size of the task. You might liken this approach to the way that many people approach home decoration: collect colour charts, then decide on a colour scheme, then buy the paint, then buy the brushes, then do the preparation, and finally do the decoration once all the background work is done and it seems manageable.

Managing stress

Stress is basically a demand made on the adaptive capacities of the mind and body. Traditionally, stress was viewed as a bad thing, to be avoided or reduced. However, this assumes that all stress is bad, which is an over-simplification. All athletes, sportspeople, actors or presenters will tell you that they cannot perform at their best unless they feel *some* stress. Literally, they need to feel the rush of adrenalin in order to achieve. If you have looked at the BBC *Raise Your Game* website (www.bbc.co.uk/wales/raiseyourgame) you will have noticed this. Likewise, many people need challenges that excite them and keep them on their toes, without which life would ultimately become dull. All these are examples of 'good stress'.

Obviously, there is also 'bad stress' – demands placed on us which we cannot meet physically or psychologically.

It is useful to be able to differentiate these, as they will vary for each person. What causes bad stress for one person can be a source of exhilaration for another. It might be useful just to identify this and, if appropriate, discuss it with a friend or colleague – or particularly with someone working in the employment sector you may be thinking of joining. You can note down your thoughts on stress in the following box.

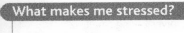

Of course, stress is not always externally imposed. People who are high-achievers often impose extremely high expectations on themselves, making themselves their own worst enemies. Is it appropriate at times to be gentler on yourself and to take more note of what you value overall in life? What are the ways in which you might be able to remove or reduce some of the negative aspects of stress?

Some employers also offer stress counselling or stress management courses. Check with your staff development office, if you have one. Some courses may be available anonymously or out of hours so that your line manager does not have to countersign your application form or agree to your attending. This can be advantageous because it may be the line manager who is causing some of the stress!

An additional source of support or advice may be your home insurance company. Many companies now have a confidential helpline that you can access 24 hours a day for advice about stress management or healthcare. Check your policy for details. Additionally, many trade unions and professional associations also provide such a service for their members. Again, check your membership pack for details.

Marketing yourself

The term marketing does not just mean selling. Yes, of course you will be selling yourself through your services, expertise or experience, perhaps to the highest bidder. But marketing is much more sophisticated than that. It involves:

* researching carefully your potential market/s
* establishing what your product/service portfolio is
* establishing a specific benefit (in quality, range, speed of service, flexibility, etc.) which no competitor can offer – your *unique selling proposition* (USP)
* establishing a specific market where what you offer is of clear value and worth.

This would be equally true whether your market is as an employee targeting an employer or as a consultant marketing his/her services. Yet the highest bidder is not necessarily the most appropriate home for your services. Before you commit yourself to one purchaser, whether it be as an employee or as a freelance or business, you would be wise to establish some 'rules of engagement'. Depending on whether you are approaching someone as an employee, as a consultant or trader, you will wish to find out what the purchaser has on offer. These would include the following.

If considering employment:
* Apart from income, what else can the employer offer me?
* What about professional or personal development?
* What about encouragement to pursue qualifications or gain additional experience?
* What amount of autonomy will I be allowed in the post?
* How much scope is there for independent thought or actions?
* Where can I aim for in the future?
* What if the company/organization contracts: how will I continue to gain the employability skills I've been developing through this book?

If considering self-employment:
Perhaps you have decided on *self-employment* or to *start a business*. As you develop your product or service portfolio, you may gain a deal with a particular customer:

* Is it a once-only deal?
* Is there the opportunity for repeat business?

* Is there scope for you to offer similar, related products or services so that the purchaser might buy a complete package?
* What facilities, services or opportunities can the purchaser provide for you which might make the work easier, more pleasant, more stimulating or reliable?
* What level of expenses will the purchaser provide or are you expected to pick up the tab for all of these?
* On what basis will the purchaser be paying? Weekly, monthly, after each 'delivery'?
* What time lag is there between delivery and payment – instant, at the end of the month, after two months?

Maintaining your employability

Having read this book, at the back of your mind should always be the question *'How do I maintain my employability?'* You will be only too aware by now that having certain skills and knowledge at one moment in time does not mean that such skills will always be sought. Knowledge and skills can atrophy and die and one must be constantly conscious of changing needs and demands, retaining flexibility and adaptability.

In order to reach the interview it is likely that you will be asked to complete some or all of the following: an application form, curriculum vitae (CV) and a letter of application. The important point to remember is that at each stage of the process you are marketing yourself. Your letter of request for the application details and forms will start your file (because organizations are always interested in assessing the number of requests that are converted into applications). If it is scrappy it is not going to create a good impression.

action planning

In this chapter you will learn: how to devise your own action plan; how to review and evaluate action plans and about what you have learned about yourself!

We'll consider briefly some of the key aspects of action planning. One of the main priorities is to be able to keep yourself in mind and to stay focused. You will need to be able to prioritize activities and to periodically maintain your own motivation by talking yourself up. We will keep on track by going for a short ride in a hot-air balloon and think about evaluating progress and considering key points. All of this can only work if you keep a focus on the most important aspect of the whole process – you.

Devising an action plan

By this stage you should feel reasonably confident about what you have discovered about yourself, your motivations, your aspirations and where you are most likely to find fulfilling and rewarding work.

However, it is very easy to let your enthusiasm and good intentions drift. So you need a structure to help you keep focused and to check whether you are achieving your objectives. This is where an **action plan** comes in. You can, for example, use it to monitor your plans, including your force field analysis. An action plan is simply a plan of action – it's no more difficult than that. But, for an action plan to work effectively, a useful mnemonic to remember is SMART. An action plan should be:

* **S**pecific
* **M**easurable
* **A**chievable
* **R**ealistic
* **T**ime-bound.

Keeping yourself in mind

You should be at the forefront of your thoughts in your planning. This is not selfishness – you have already identified those others who are dear to you and for whom you have responsibilities. You are already taking their needs into account in your planning. Furthermore, by being pro-active, you are taking much more control of the situation than just waiting for things to happen to you (and to them) over which you have no control.

However, it is easy to get deflected from your plans and to let time catch up. To help overcome this you will find it beneficial to keep a clear note of:

* your intentions
* your plans
* your targets.

Prioritizing activities

If you want to get the most out of life, you will be seeking new opportunities and challenges. Sometimes, there may be too many to choose from and so you will have to consider 'Which of these should I pick?' You may need to remind yourself of your core purpose, of what you really want to achieve.

Talking yourself up

Making decisions to change fundamental aspects of your life or to retain the same position but with a different perspective on life can be hard. The value of having someone with whom you can talk openly has already been stressed. Vital also is the quality of feedback that you get from others. But you also need feedback from yourself, to motivate you by recognizing what you have achieved and how you can meet your targets. The following tips can help:

* Identify your continuing achievements.
* Quantify the progress you have made.
* Reflect on what you have done and ask yourself: 'In order to carry out that task, what skills and abilities do I have?' Likewise, ask yourself: 'What do I need to be good at to do this?'
* List your skills and abilities!

Take the time to talk to yourself. This could be while sitting at traffic lights, on the train home or as you go to sleep. You can do so silently if necessary! Say 'Well done', give yourself a metaphorical pat on the back and take pride in what you have done. In other words, as the saying goes, 'Make an appointment with yourself'.

Keeping on track

You might like to think about the decisions you have made for your journey as being like planning a journey by hot-air balloon (see Figure 12). It's your idea – your release from what you are

Figure 12 *What do you need for a successful hot-air balloon journey?*

doing now. You are the force to provide lift-off – but you have to show that it's more than hot air.

It's you who is doing the planning for the journey – you are planning your route, your supplies, the distance to travel and the duration of the journey. Is it a long-distance trip? Are you in it for the duration? Do you want to see what the journey is like before you commit yourself to a long-haul? You are also considering the altitude you wish to travel at – how high do you want to go?

You also need to check while you are preparing your balloon that it is securely tethered to the ground – that there is security. But at the point of lift-off you need to cut those ties and gradually jettison that ballast. What is your plan for this?

During the planning you'll need to take into account the expert opinion of others about the equipment and supplies you will need. You'll need to budget to determine the likely cost (in financial and other terms). You would be wise to get a meteorologist's forecast for the conditions you are likely to encounter. You will also need the forecast during the journey so that you can avoid extreme conditions or turbulence. You will need to consider who you are taking along for the ride and what contribution they are going to make to the journey – and what they are going to gain from it. You will need to keep in touch with someone whose feet are firmly on the ground – your ground crew or observer.

In summary:

* What and who do you need in the basket?
* What and who is providing the lift-off?
* Who and what are the ties to the ground?
* Who will be your expert?
* Who will be your meteorologist?
* Who, if anyone, will be your passenger/s?
* Who will you keep in contact with to report on progress?
* What might make the balloon crash or fly off-course?

Evaluating progress

Such motivational small-talk as described in 'Talking yourself up' may not always be easy and you should not get carried away with false praise.

Things will not always go well and you need to have the courage to evaluate your own progression and to improve any shortcomings in your own expectations of yourself.

Evaluating by considering key points

* Keep your targets in mind and review them regularly.
* Praise your achievements.
* Evaluate where and why some things have not gone so well.
* Identify the causes of this.
* Try to remedy the situation by setting achievable targets.
* If necessary, be realistic and revise your targets or time-scales.

Action points

The action points below are *your* future!

Postscript

At times things will be difficult. You may feel alone, and the responsibility for the decisions you make may weigh heavily on you. But, ultimately, you will have the satisfaction of knowing that you have taken more control of your life, and that whatever decisions you make, they are ones with which you can live. This feeling is eloquently expressed in the poem *The Road Not Taken* by the American poet Robert Frost:

> **Two roads diverged in a wood, and I –**
> **I took the one less travelled by,**
> **and that has made all the difference.**
>
> From *The Poetry of Robert Frost*,
> edited by Edward Connery Latham (Jonathan Cape)

Whichever decision you make, you know that it is based on what you now understand about yourself and where you want to go. Whichever road you take – well-worn or less travelled by – enjoy it.